© 2020 Divine Works Publishing LLC.

Sandy Ground Tales: Fisher Men

ALL RIGHTS RESERVED. No part of this publication may be reproduced, stored in a retrieval system, or transmitted in any form or by any means, electronic, mechanical, photocopying, recording or otherwise without the prior permission of the publisher or in accordance with the provisions of the Copyright, Designs, and Patents Act 1988 or under the terms of any license permitting limited copying issued by the Copyright Licensing Agency.

Printed in the United States of America,
Divine Works Publishing, LLC
Royal Palm Beach, Florida USA
First Edition: October 22, 2024

ISBN 13: 978-1-949105-73-5 (Paperback)
ISBN 13: 978-1-949105-74-2 (Hardback)
ISBN 13: 978-1-949105-75-9 (eBook)

www.DivineWorksPublishing.com
561-990-BOOK (2665)

CONTENTS

Introduction 4
Fisher Man – Ed Arose 5
FYI 32
Mind Games 34
Morals of the Story 34
Fisher of Man – No Greater Love 35
FYI 88
Mind Games 90
Morals of the Story 90
About the Scribe 92

INTRODUCTION

Fisher Men – the second book in the Sandy Ground Tales Series. This book is a compilation of two riveting and uniquely illustrated stories filled with creatively woven images, facts and juxtapositions. From the shores of Sandy Ground, Anguilla, Fisher Men sails through the real life inspirational stories of Ed Carty and Aristo Richardson.

Bathed in thrill and pivoting around themes of tragedy, bravery, hope, leadership and brotherly love, the book resounds with the core Anguillian values of determination, hard work, courage, love for country and self-sacrifice.

Fisher Men possesses the capacity to inspire the young, engage the academic, intrigue the philosopher, excite the historian and catch leisurely readers hook, line & sinker.

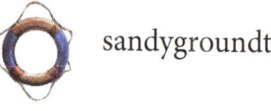 sandygroundtales@gmail.com
@sgtseries

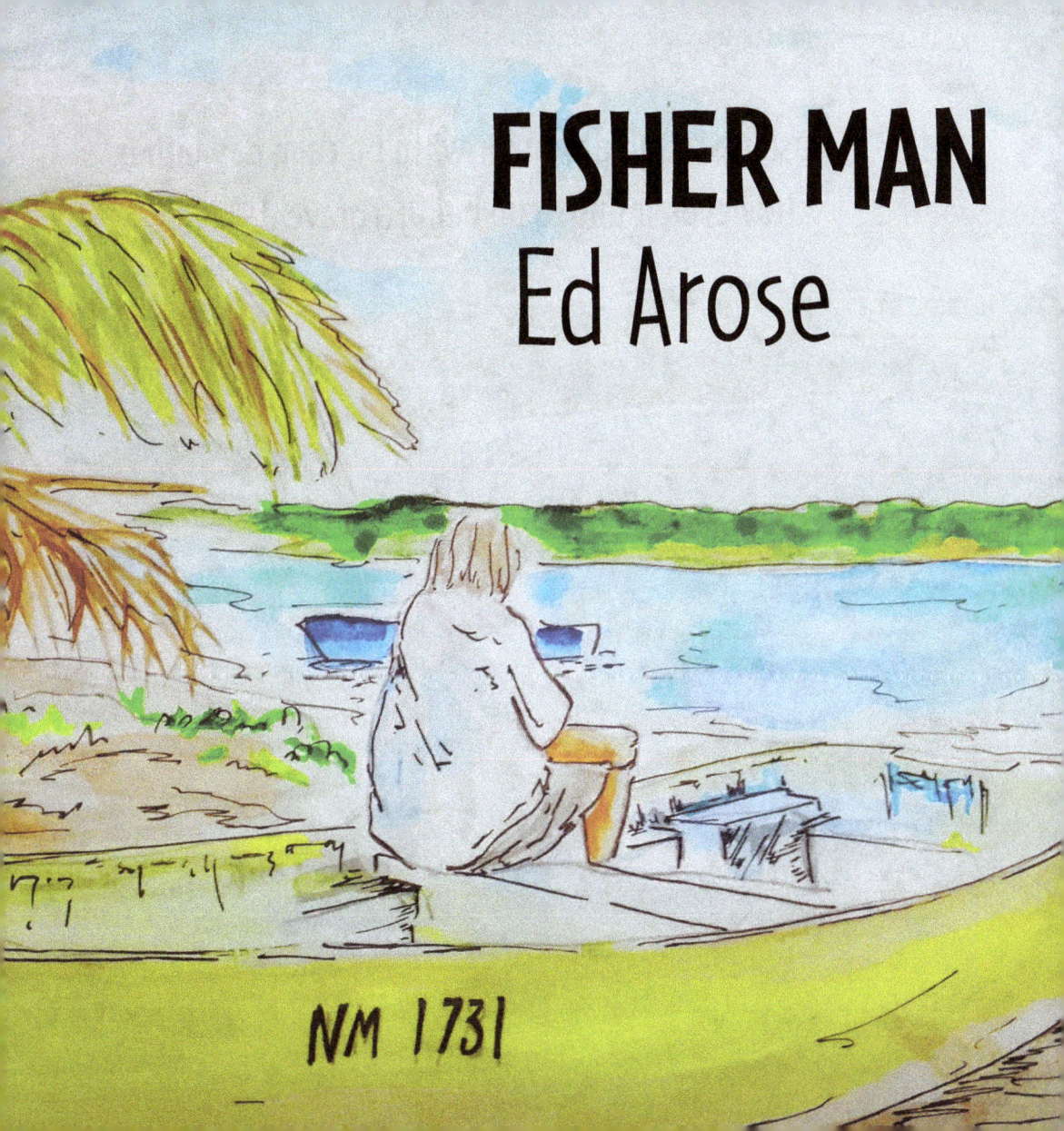

It wasn't a rough day but it wasn't a calm day either. However, it ended up being a grave day.

Antonio was all set to go out fishing with the boys, in a boat that he was so proud of. It was a big coble boat, which had lug-sails, powered by sweeps. It had a live well inside...probably the first one on the island with that. He called it the 'Olivia C'.

From Road Bay Port, Antonio had captained schooners around the USVI, BVI and ABC islands. He knew the Silky waters of the Leeward and Windward Islands like the back of his hand, inside out.

He had sailed through the archipelago more than Columbus, but like all other Anguillian fisher men, fishing in Anguilla waters was his pride and joy, especially fishing out in the North.

As a skilled and experienced captain and boss fisher man he always Frilled a boat. Yet, he never owned the Whitetip or Blacktip of one. Shame.

But his son William, aka Uncle, who use to wash out, hang out, and ball up his cotton fishing lines every Sunday for Monday fishing, was determined he would wuk like a Bull to change that. And he did.

He sent the money. It was done. He had fulfilled his dream of helping his father own his own boat.

So every time Antonio went out in Olivia C, it was with Oceanic joy. He took guys in the North many a time and taught them the fishing ropes. Joel and Gorton tagged along this time.

They had all the necessary coutremenaats, including the all-important three fire rocks johnny cakes.

Uncle Neddy was supposed to join them too but his daughter, Meridith, didn't get up in time to make his johnny cakes.

So, he sent a message saying he wasn't going again. 'Cause a man can't survive out on dem seas without someting holding him in his stomach eh!

The plan, as normal, was to go in the North
and come back as usual, by sunset.
It did not come to pass.
After sunset, all of Sandy Ground, South Hill and
North Hill knew that something was terribly wrong.

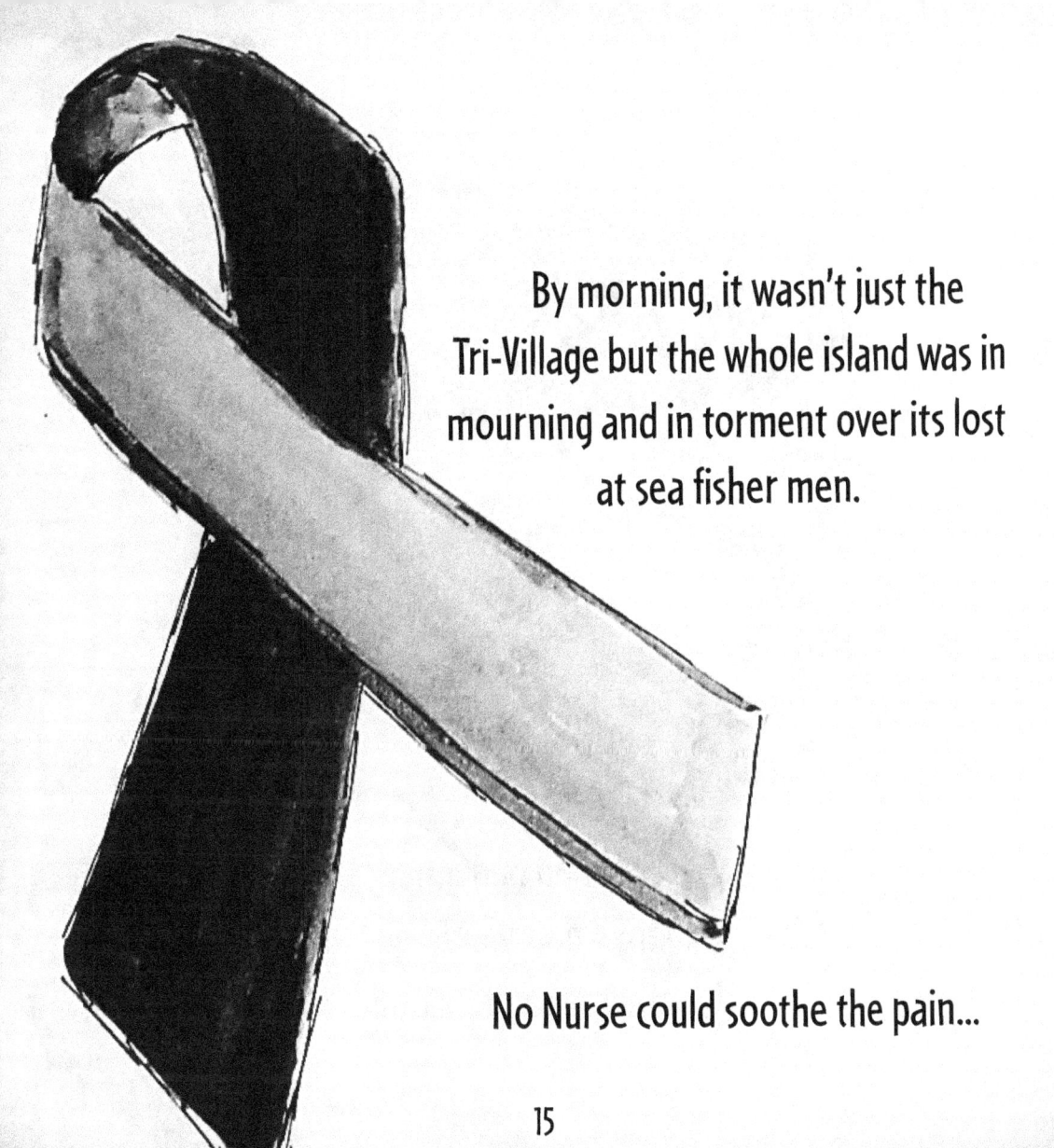

By morning, it wasn't just the Tri-Village but the whole island was in mourning and in torment over its lost at sea fisher men.

No Nurse could soothe the pain...

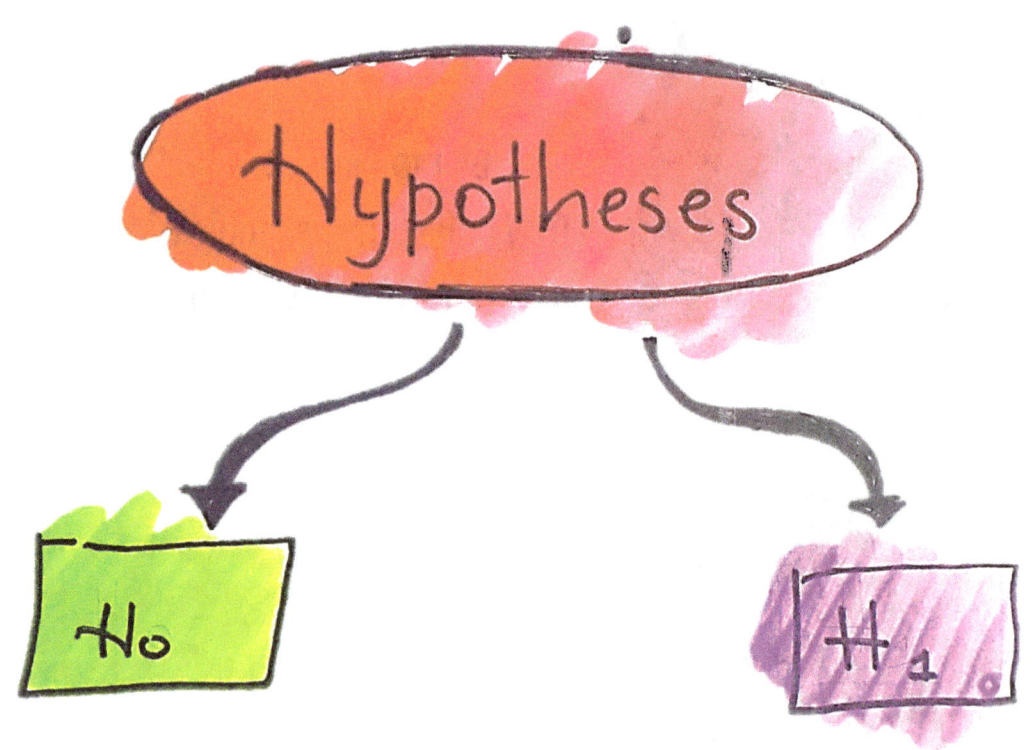

What had happened?
Way too many unanswered questions.
Hypotheses can't be done.

At foreday morning, a few boats sailed out to look, but not too far out.

The fear of the North rose up, as their Goliath. It began to besiege Anguilla and its fisher folk. For what seemed like donkey years, but was just a few, it defied them every day, seemingly saying, "Come out here if ayah bad nuh! Come if ayah bad!"

The fisher men in their own eyesight began seeing themselves as powerless grasshoppers.

The Anguillians,
once bitten by the invisible Goblin in the North,
were now twice shy.
They played it safe and stayed close to their Greenland.
When Sunshine City mountains began leaving sight,
that was the signal to turn back!

It pained dem ya see! Because for over 200 nautical miles to the North, was their waters. This sea water was in their blood.
It was burning dem.

The handful of seasoned fisher men shouted
"Aye, Aye, Captain!"
Cool like a Lemon, Ed had gotten the breakthrough!

Many with fluttering hearts and praying lips watched them
leave de Bay. Some shaking dem heads said,
"Dem struppid, crazy fools." "Go to ayah death."
On the other hand, the Megamouth champions
yelled every last piece of advice they could
(even though they had little, if anything, to back their chat).
Others, couldn't bear to come Bayside.

Five hours later, there were Great White size shouts and applause to welcome dem back into de Bay!
With one throw, David..., sorry, Ed had knocked Goliath out cold, cold and chopped off his head.

The next day, every fisher man whose heart was yearning for the big Blue in the North, as if it was the burial place of his navel string, was heading out dere.

The invisible giant Basking in the North, had fallen to Ed. The Anguillian fisher men, like Tigers, boldly charged towards the North with their fishing artillery to finish slaying any of Goliath's siblings who would have been still lurking around.

Free at last, Free at last, Thank God Almighty they were free again, to go in the North, at last!
The siege in Anguilla was over because, Ed arose.

FYI

Antonio Connor, from South Hill, Joel Connor from Sandy Ground and Gorton Carty from South Hill were lost on 16 March, 1963. The sun sat that evening with young and old at Baby Coleman Hill on the South Hill, looking, hoping, wishing that something, anything looking like a boat would begin to come into sight. With no electricity on the island, everyone had to go home by night fall...with fallen hearts.

William Connor, better known as Michael or Uncle, was Antonio's eldest son. At 91 years old residing in Anguilla and he still remembered the pain of that phone call on that grave day, 61 years ago this year, 2024. Uncle passed shortly before this work could be printed.

Joel Connor's daughter, Celestia Connor, was only 7 months at the time. So unlike Uncle, she has no personal recollection of her father but she does have one picture of him, which she holds dearly.

Cossilda O'Loughlin, better known as Cossie, along with her 4 siblings are some of the living grandchildren of the third lost soul, Gorton Carty.

Uncle Neddy's correct name was John Richardson. One wonders if Meridith had gotten licks that morning for not waking up in time to do the johnny cakes? She was the mother of Rodney and Hilton Richardson of Sandy Ground. Her other children Joshua, Bell and Ruth have passed.

Ed's unmatched fishing prowess continues and up to today, Anguilla's waters still pull him out several times a week to be who he was born to be, a Fisher Man.

MIND GAMES

- List all the species of sharks which are embedded in the story.
- Explain to or ask someone how johnny cakes are baked on three fire rocks.
- Name the two biblical stories that are used as allusions in the story.
- Ask around for names and general information of Anguillian fisher men who were lost at sea over the years. Send your list to: sandygroundtales@gmail.com.

Morals of the story:
1. Face it, to conquer it!
2. ....
3. ....
4. ....

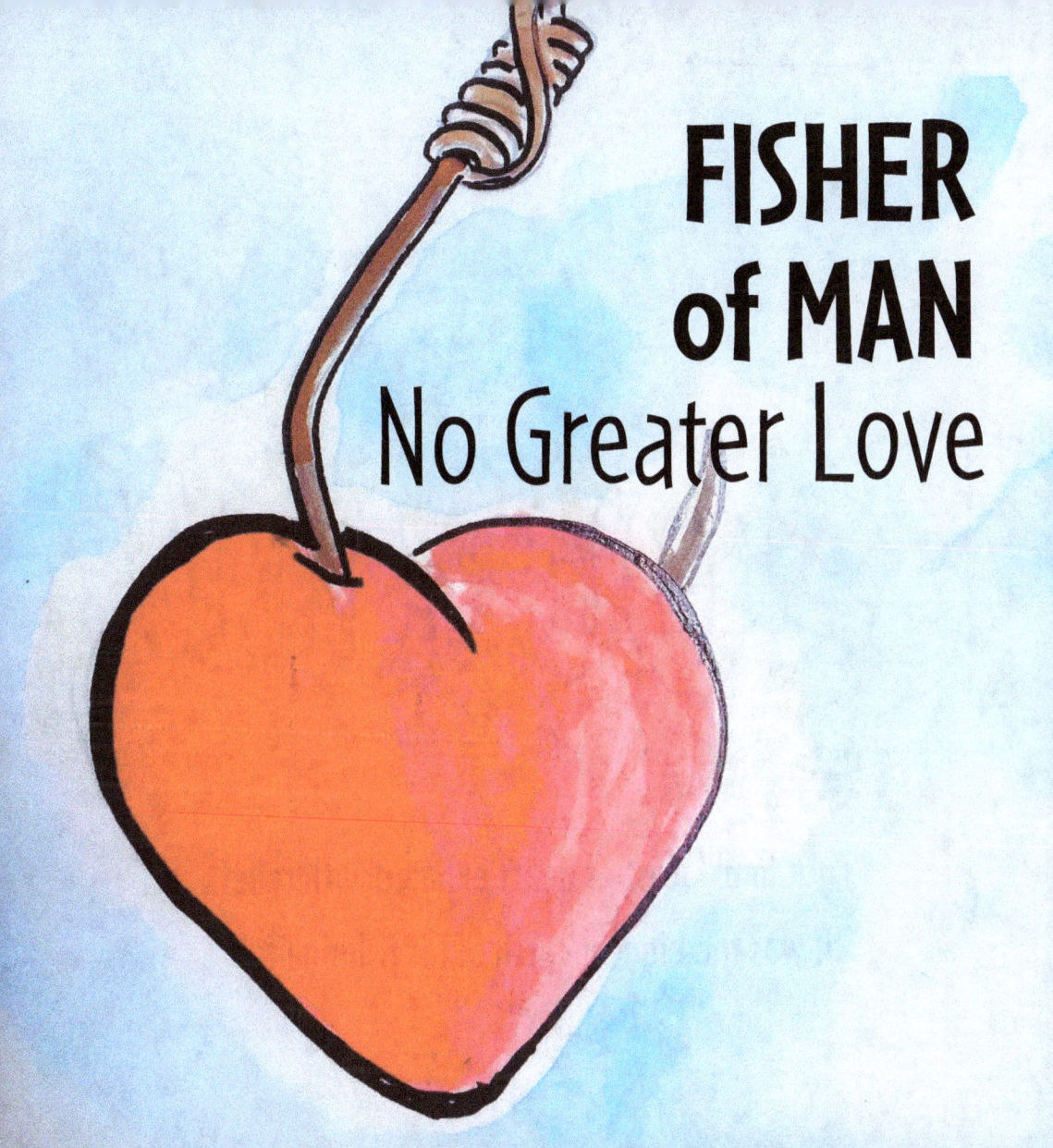

I got him

"I got him!" Aristo's heart exhaled with relief.
It was the biggest catch of his fishing life!

Many years before Aristo caught a fish named Sam, when he was about 9 years old, he would leave Sandy Ground to go down Sandy with his father Lindsay and other men, to fish.
One man on each side of the boat rowed.

A next, stood up in the middle of the transom and used the third oar which stood upright in a hole carved out for sculling.

Once the wind hit, going down-wind to Sandy was Bliss. The sculling would then act more like a tiller because the guys didn't have to row. Aristo mother's shower curtain was the sail. It was hung end to end on the two oars that were then not in use. They would be outside Sandy in no time...pure Joy. When the wind from the Nord (North) East hit dat plastic, it was Euphoria!

His father showed him the ropes and made him the engine man. That gave Aristo the leeway to take up the boat any time. He preferred the nights so he could be alone. The calm and peace with well-lit skies made for cool nights. Something mysterious, unexpected and amazing always showed up out there.

In his teenage days, he began tag teaming with Sam from Island Harbour. They met playing hard ball cricket against each other in the local league and both were good enough to occasionally travel overseas on the National Youth Team.

They became true friends...congruent. Sam showed Aristo how to make funnels, baskets, traps, pots - all the coutrements. And it was Aristo's boat Sam used for months one time when his was down. They not only shared knowledge, bait, and resources but they also fished with each other too.

One time, Aristo even took Sam with him down to Tuna Bank. Yep, 20 miles west south west of Anguilla, under the sea, is a mountain that rises from the sand base of about 400 fathoms deep to 108 fathoms upwards to its peak...the tunas bank there!

They became true friends...congruent. Sam showed Aristo how to make funnels, baskets, traps, pots - all the coutrements. And it was Aristo's boat Sam used for months one time when his was down. They not only shared knowledge, bait, and resources but they also fished with each other too.

One time, Aristo even took Sam with him down to Tuna Bank. Yep, 20 miles west south west of Anguilla, under the sea, is a mountain that rises from the sand base of about 400 fathoms deep to 108 fathoms upwards to its peak...the tunas bank there!

That spot makes for a great home for migratory pelagic fish. The tunas know this and so they come to feed on them and so too, the humans come to complete the food chain.

Sam had the understanding that for Aristo, fishing is done with on de fly algorithms. Aristo, he just goes with his Pythegras flows.

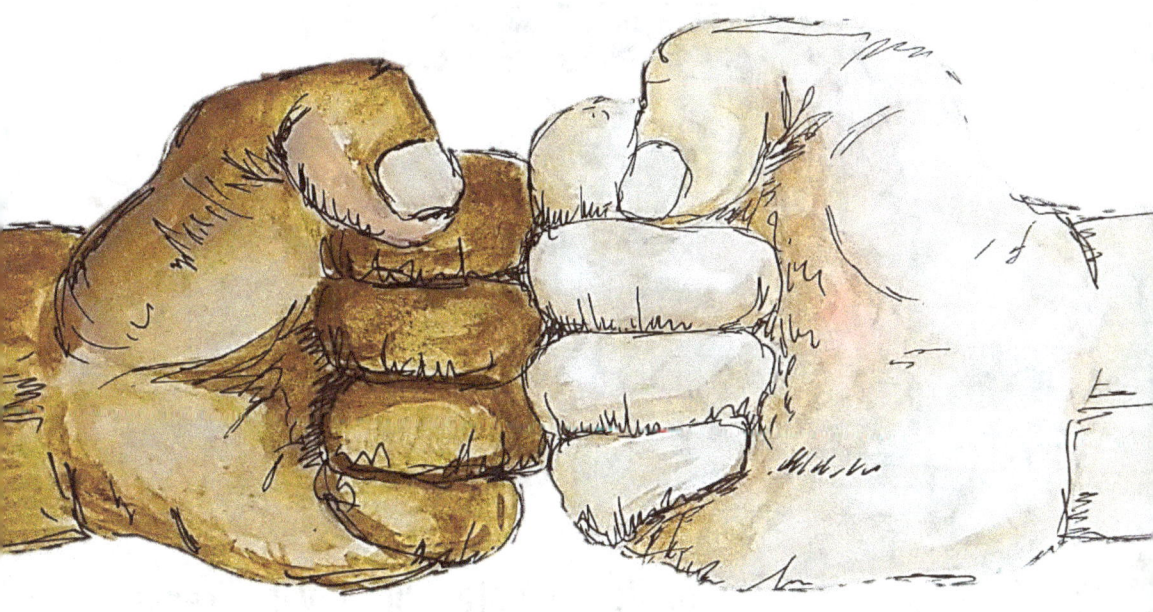

Aristo would leave shore destined for one spot but change he mind because he had a re-calculation based on his analyses of the elements (and recalibration of his gut)!
Dem guys were tight.

A few months after Aristo had gotten his driver's license and hadn't hit a stroke since, he came home from long lining to find an early Christmas gift from Sam parked in his grandmodder yard up North Hill. It turned out to be a Chevrolet truck. It was Aristo's first vehicle!

Over the years, when he wasn't out 50 miles in de Nord of Anguilla long line fishing, struggling with unliftable 10 foot sharks or penning boat loads of jacks, Aristo was out in the Nord drift fishing on the bank...
he loved this low maintenance fishing.

Once upwind, the boat, unpropelled, was left to drift with the current and swaying with the tide. They would catch the hinds, old wife and butterfish who were out for their morning feed, on lines with hooks baited with soldier crabs and bigger bait like redman, whitening, or horse eye. No fuss, just drift across the bank, catch fish and sail back upwind and
then drift down again.

Over the years, when he wasn't out 50 miles in de Nord of Anguilla long line fishing, struggling with unliftable 10 foot sharks or penning boat loads of jacks, Aristo was out in the Nord drift fishing on the bank...
he loved this low maintenance fishing.

Once upwind, the boat, unpropelled, was left to drift with the current and swaying with the tide. They would catch the hinds, old wife and butterfish who were out for their morning feed, on lines with hooks baited with soldier crabs and bigger bait like redman, whitening, or horse eye. No fuss, just drift across the bank, catch fish and sail back upwind and then drift down again.

Sam's favourite place for setting his lobster pots, and a few fish pots for silks, was on the edge of The Deep. This is straight up over Scrub, going south and east. He always started pulling his 100 plus pots at the head of the lines which were set on an angle. This helped him find them easy as the fishing grounds above Scrub are beyond large. In that order, one by one, he pulled, and filled baskets.

Sam pulled several times a week, most times by his lonesome. Each time Aristo went with Sam, Aristo noted his predictable moves and mannerisms. This modus operandi intrigued Aristo.

One day, 14 March, 2008 to be exact, Aristo needed to get at some lobster traps he had set on a bank just 12 to 15 minutes or so, just outside of Scrub. And of course, he asked Sam to carry him. The agreement was that Sam would go out the marnin' for heself, then come back in a lil' early, around four or so and then carry Aristo to pull his handful of pots.

Aristo packed up his gear, lobster bait etc. In his truck and was waiting on Sam's call. 4 o'clock came, no call. 5 o'clock came, no call. So, he figure Sam changed his mind.

Aristo slept that moon light Friday night and Sam did not call.

Well, the Satruday marnin' while Aristo was on the Rev. Leonard Carty Drive, heading to Sandy Ground, he tuned into Hammer. It was a live conversation about a fisher man who went out to sea and his empty boat was found, but not him.

Aristo head swell right up!

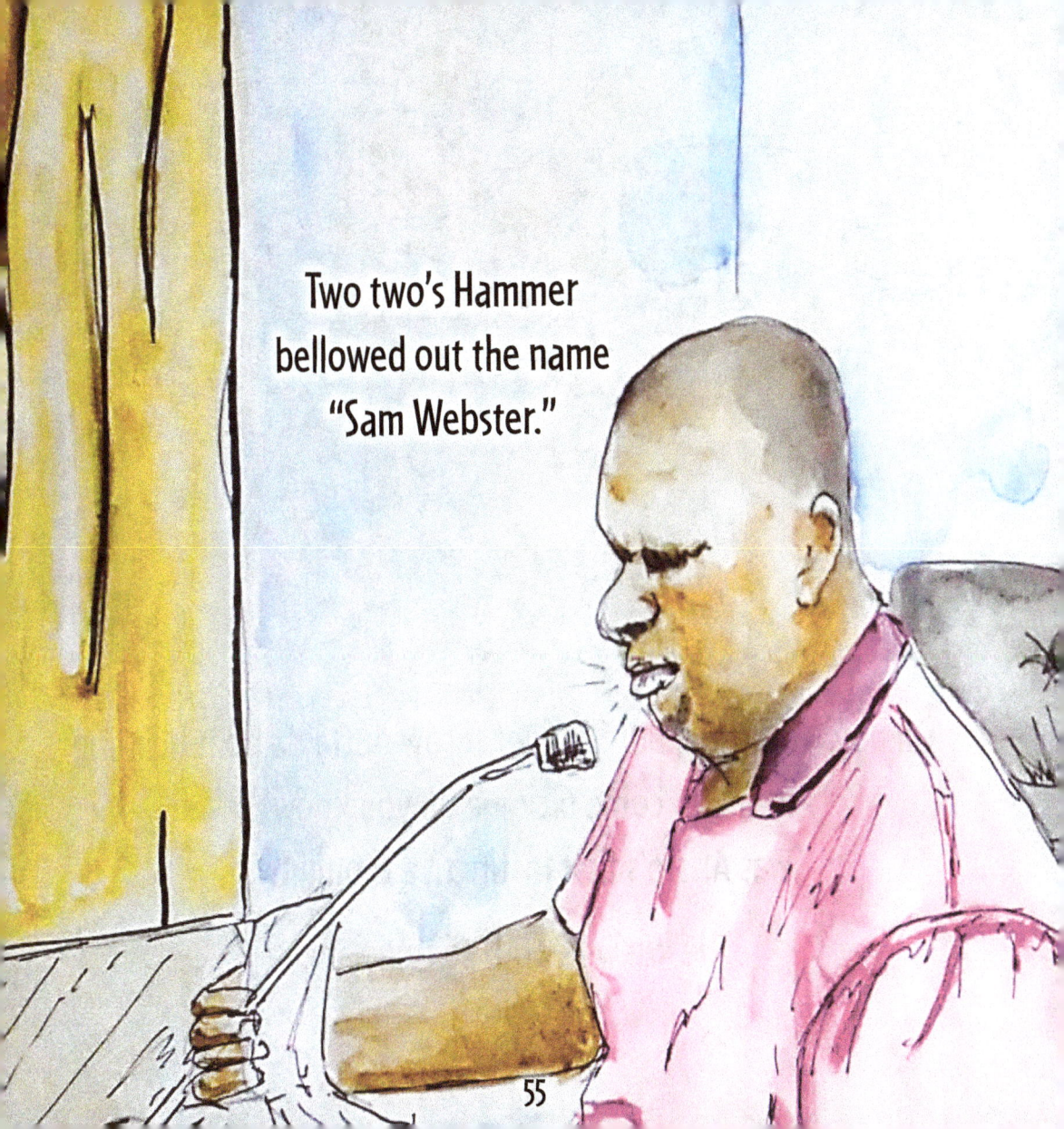

'Oh boy, 'tis noting but Sam get throw outta da boat hustling trying to come pick me up you know' was Aristo's first instinctive thought.

He knew he HAD to find Sam.

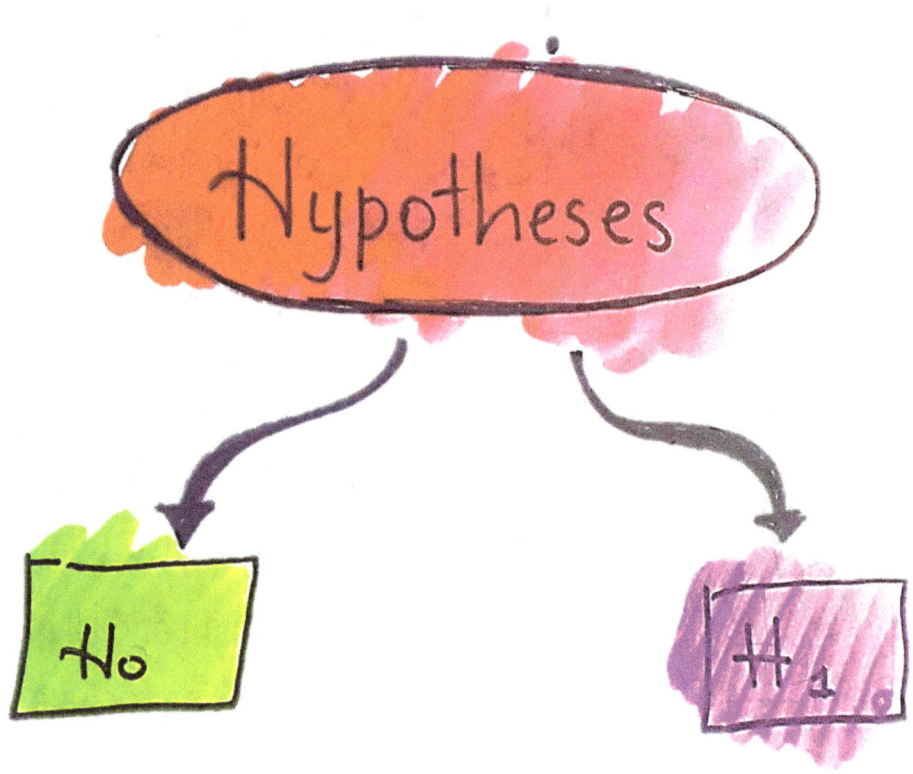

What had happened?
Way too many unanswered questions.
Hypotheses can't done.

"Where is the boat?" Aristo asked as he walked on the noisy panicky jetty. He was told it was already at the police station in Sandy Ground. He was hoping he could get the GPS tracking data to inform and support his hypothesis.

He strongly felt that once Sam was pitched from the boat, it would have sent it in circles, and the GPS data would show the coordinates from where the circular motion would have begun, along with its velocity. With that information, he would work his equation from there.

But his request was denied. So Aristo had to come up with another method.

Jus' then, The Fisheries boat, Cobra 2, was coming in to dock up and dem boys was hag right out. Ya could see the tiredness and the distraught in dem eyes from being out all night and marnin' and from not having caught Sam.

The sea water had dem beat!

Aristo went to dem and talked them through his logic. Then he barefoot self, had the gall to open his mouth to give motivational TED Talk 1, "We gah go back up dere look for eem." He had to raise their logarithm.

Their faces went even whiter looking at irrational Aristo.
'Nahhh boy, we dog tired and plus
we ain't got no more gas' they blurted out.
Louvan, who had recently arrived, suck he teeth and bawl out
his command, 'Man wa foolishness ayou talkin'! Go in de Long
Pa' and get wha'ever gas ayah need! Tell um, I sen' ayah!"
And he suck his teeth again.

So de guys,
Carlos, Mitchy and Percy
breathe hard and eat and drink a
lil' while somebody followed the
General's orders and got the gas!
They fueled up the boat and
pessimistically headed back out...
"It's like looking for a needle in a
haystack" they kept repeating in
Aristo ears....and like a stuck
record he would respond,
"Da mean dat we have a
chance then, right?"

Aristo, based on his experience from drift fishing in using the current, wind speed and wind direction, calculated that based on where the boat was found drifting, that Sam would have had to be thrown out of his boat somewhere close to his pots.

So with Aristo now calling the shots on the rescue boat,
he shared the plan. They were going to the head of Sam pots,
which position he knew well, and start the search there,
continuing down the angle of all his pots,
just in case he was hol'ing on to one of them.
And then go out to the Nord where
the empty vessel was found,
which was quite a distance
from Scrub.

So heading up to Sam's first pot, east and south of Scrub, they cut through the channel where the waters from The Deep rise because of hitting the shallower land, for about 3 miles it's rough seas. There the SXM Dutch Coast Guard helicopter and RIB boat were visible. They had company. This brought a few smiles and gave the guys a much-needed energy boost.

Dem went up, dem went up, dem went up, dem went up and saw nothing looking like Sam.
They got to the top of his pots and, nothing.

The agreed consensus was that it had a general north current. So Aristo focused for a while and did his maths again. He calculated that it would have been around 16 hours that Sam was now drifting, taking into consideration the time when they found the boat. And at a distance of ¼ mile an hour that would put him like 4 miles out to the north.

So his new plan now was for them to fine teeth comb that entire area going down. He figure that if he knew Sam, which he did, Sam would relax himself and not fight the current too hard, and this would cause him to stay alive and drift in a north westerly direction.

So he told the guys the new plan was now to search in a diagonal course, 4 miles out to the north come down and in, and do it not in a big way.

So they went to the high north to start.

16 hrs × ¼ miles per hr = 4 miles

COMMU NICATION

But with no direct communication links with the SXM chopper and RIB, the results of Aristo's graphing calculator could not be relayed to them.

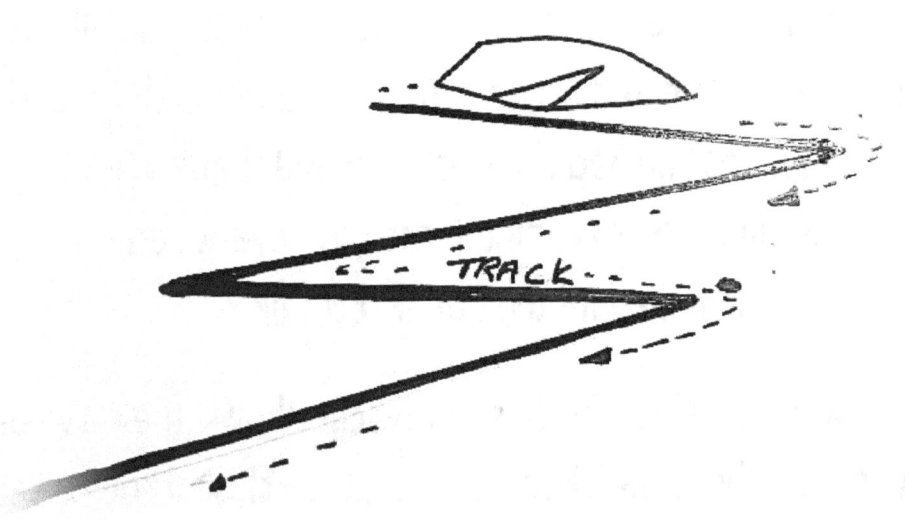

The boat captain followed Aristo's directives and from just about 15 degrees from Nord, they went out diagonally to a 3 ½ to 4 miles end point, then come back in 3 then went back out another 3 ½ to 4 miles, then come back in again and so forth, all at about 12 to 14 knots.

After about the 2nd time, the negative faces and vibes started to flow again and Aristo had to be quick on his barefeet. Factoring in that he had the fresh legs and that it was only adrenaline was keeping these guys eyes open, he nailed motivational TED Talk 2.

"Boys when you look at those TV rescue shows, the survivors always say the boat was right dere, it was so close, I coulda see you, I was waving at them, I was doing this, I was doing that..... So boys, I can't give up. You all relax and leave me run de boat'. There was a sigh from the guys and with that, obtuse Aristo took command of the wheel too.

After about the 5th Doh Doh run, when they were heading back towards Anguilla land, midpoint on the southern end of Aristo search area, the boys started verbalizing the wear and tear on their bodies and mind, again. They had no more to give.

It was now almost 24 hours they were on the open water. Forcefully now, they began insisting, "It's a needle in a haystack, Aristo. We tell ya so from de start. We ain't gone find eem. Let's go home, we don't know where we goin' or wha we doing!"

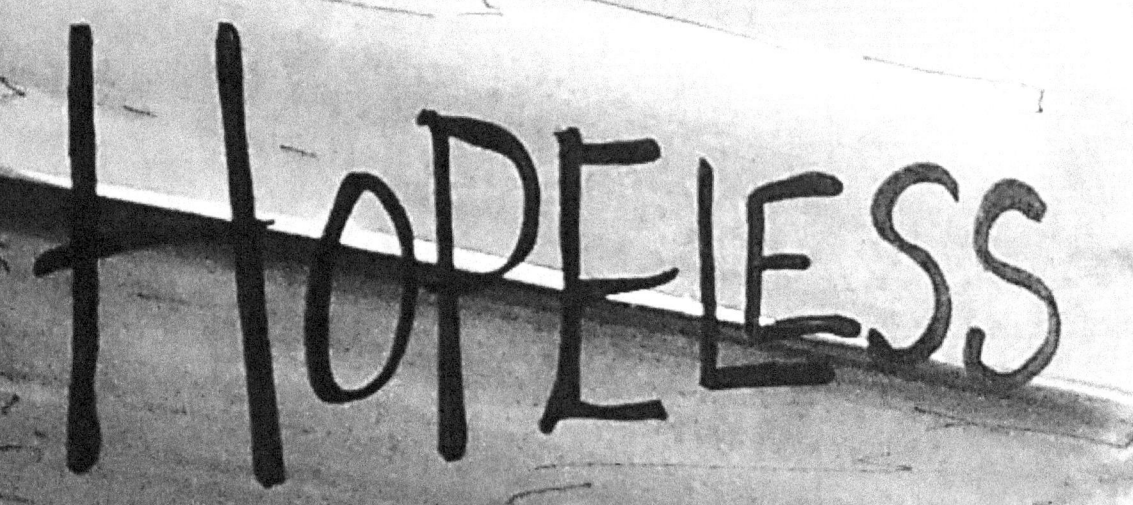

Aristo saw that they had reached their full limit and gave in but before he did, he pulled out the Hail Mary he had saving up jus' for this moment. "We gune go Nord fi jus' one more run and we gune do it fas' fas' at full throttle, say 20 knots."

They agreed, finally knowing they would be on land soon in this event.

Aristo looked up at the blue skies and silently prayed.

Aristo throttled up the boat about 20 knots and run her and run her and run her to the Nord to get out at least 4 miles. Just when he was about to stop and turn around, he said to himself, "Let mi go a lil' fudda" and he run her faster still.

When he felt a release in his spirit (gut), he slowed down the boat to almost idling and while making the turn to come back to face Anguilla direction, with everything inside of him, from the bottom of his barefoot up, Aristo bellowed out motivational TED Talk 3.

"Sam, Sam, put up ya hands;
Sam, Sam put up ya hands;
Put up your hands in the air,
Let's see ya, Sam!"

Right den and dere, all of a sudden Sam couso bawl out,
"Boy, look eem dere! Look eem dere!".

"Look eem dere fi true!"

"Aya looka wuk!"

"Where?"

"Tank ya Jesus!"

"Where?"

"You gotta be joken"

Raucousness erupted in the boat!!
"God bless our eyesight!"

Aristo's trigonometry had worked out on point! The bow of the boat was pointing directly at Sam about 400 metres away. There he was, throwing up his hands and buoys in the air! (Those were his hold or die buoys that were covered in insects, vicious algae and stinger nettle which he had bitten off and loosed from pots, and held on to for dear, dear life. Some he had forced under his shirt to float him, which he was now launching like fireworks). Sam's time of intense worship, prayer and fasting was rewarded.

Fully strengthened, the captain jumped up and took back command of the vessel and throttled up towards Sam. Once some feet away, Aristo jumped into the Nord and swam to Sam. He caught and held Sam, hugged Sam and said, "I love you".

Sam responded, "I knew you wouldna give up on me Aristo. I knew it."

The now revived guys threw them a rope and pulled them in. Once inside the boat, Aristo sat on the floor with weathered Sam resting his head on his chest.
With that padding, after drinking some water, Sam managed to fall asleep with Aristo holding him in his arms all the way home in a boat full of animated high energy sea men!

The jubilant call to report the outcome that 'the unbelievable needle in a haystack was found alive' was made and an ambulance requested at Island Harbour, again. The ambulance was a'ready on dat same wharf jus' de day before. It had come to pick up lifeless Keith, another couso, whose heart, sea legs, and entire body fainted out in the Nord when he and others found Sam's life-less boat a drift.

Even before hitting Scilly, the guys saw that it wasn't only Aristo who had come to the East from the West dat day, but all, and ah mean all, of August Monday had followed him too!

The ambulance, amidst all the jubilant sardines, got Sam and took him to the Princess Alexandra Hospital, joining Keith. A 16 mile by 3 ½ mile perimeter blanket of relief covered the island. Thank ya Jesusss!!

But aways, about a furlong, before docking up to the jetty, upon seeing the peas and corn on the wharf, Aristo did his maths one more time and calculated the fastest way to depart Island Harbour. He went with a new tangent.

He released Sam, jumped overboard, swam to shore, wordlessly walked straight to his Chevy and resumed the journey to Sandy Ground that he had started about 6 hours before. He, whom he loved, was safe...Greater Love Hath No Man Than This, That A Man Lay Down His Life For His Friend.

FYI

Survival in shark infested waters is possible. Knowing that sharks, who are one of the best hunters in the world, hunt by sound and smell would help to improve one's chances of survival, if it ever becomes necessary.

Sharks are keen vibration sensors. They are attracted to objects moving in irregular distressful patterns, like frantic splashing. These vibrations will cause sharks to come and check things out. A normal swimmer's rhythm does not attract sharks, as these vibrations do not depict a struggling/drowning/helpless pattern.

Therefore, first tip:
Do not panic and splash around in fright.
Relax.
(*LOL, easier said than done*).

Secondly, it is estimated that sharks can smell one drop of blood from a ¼ mile away. Using Aristo maths, that makes their sense of smell 10,000 times better than ours.

Therefore, second tip:
Try not to cut yourself.
(Ingesting blood from a small wound might be wise
but what if ya have a big gash?
Then, all you can do is pray that the sharks
do not like your blood type...
and could be, just like Sam,
you might find out that prayer wuks).

MIND GAMES

- List the names of the Sandy Island shuttle boats embedded in the story.
- How many mathematical terms can you identify in the story?
  HINT: There are way over thirty.
- How long is a furlong?
- How many fathoms can you free dive?

Morals of the story:
1. Never give up on those you love!
2. ....
3. ....
4. ....

About the Scribe

With roots in Sandy Ground and a continued affiliation with the village, **Avenella Griffith** has a high appreciation for its milieu. She tells these Tales in a drive to capture, for generations to come, the lives and stories of some of the people who have shaped the village. The preservation of Anguilla's great people, stories, history and traditions through inspirational writings is her broader motivation for this work.

Amongst other things, Avenella also hopes that through the Tales, people, especially boys, would enjoy reading, would dream, and be inspired to work hard to achieve their dreams.

sandygroundtales@gmail.com
@sgtseries

www.ingramcontent.com/pod-product-compliance
Lightning Source LLC
Chambersburg PA
CBHW081501070526
44586CB00019B/2450